In Love with Labs

BRETT LONGLEY

HARVEST HOUSE PUBLISHERS

EUGENE, OREGON

In Love with Labs

Copyright © 2008 by Harvest House Publishers
Eugene, Oregon 97402
www.harvesthousepublishers.com

ISBN-13: 978-0-7369-2156-5
ISBN-10: 0-7369-2156-7

Artwork © 2008 by Brett Longley and used by Harvest House Publishers, Inc., under authorization.
For more information regarding art prints featured in this book,
please contact Brett Longley at dogguy@mac.com.

Design and production by Garborg Design Works, Savage, Minnesota

Harvest House Publishers has made every effort to trace the ownership of all poems and quotes. In the event of a question arising from the use of a poem or quote, we regret any error made and will be pleased to make the necessary correction in future editions of this book.

Unattributed quotes are written by Brett Longley.

Printed in China

08 09 10 11 12 13 14 / LP / 10 9 8 7 6 5 4 3 2 1

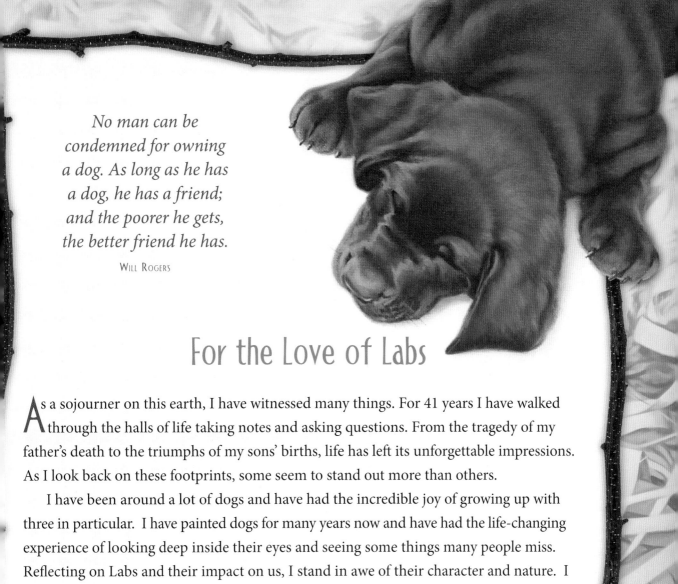

No man can be condemned for owning a dog. As long as he has a dog, he has a friend; and the poorer he gets, the better friend he has.

WILL ROGERS

For the Love of Labs

As a sojourner on this earth, I have witnessed many things. For 41 years I have walked through the halls of life taking notes and asking questions. From the tragedy of my father's death to the triumphs of my sons' births, life has left its unforgettable impressions. As I look back on these footprints, some seem to stand out more than others.

I have been around a lot of dogs and have had the incredible joy of growing up with three in particular. I have painted dogs for many years now and have had the life-changing experience of looking deep inside their eyes and seeing some things many people miss. Reflecting on Labs and their impact on us, I stand in awe of their character and nature. I have yet to enjoy the full experience of being owned by a Lab, but I can say that I have been deeply impacted by their presence. My hope is to give you a little glimpse into this amazing dog from the eyes of a dog artist. Enjoy!

The ancestor of the Labrador retriever was the St. John's retriever, a smaller version of the Newfoundland. These dogs were brought to England, probably on fishing boats. Gamekeepers crossed these Canadian imports with various breeds of gun dogs, always striving to improve the breed's hunting and retrieving instincts. By the middle of the nineteenth century, the Labrador's characteristic water-resistant coat and otter tail were already apparent. By the late 1880s, the breed was sufficiently distinctive that "Labrador retriever" became the generally accepted name of the breed. Originally black, the first recorded yellow Labrador appeared in a litter born in 1899. Chocolates were also recorded at about the same time, but never achieved the same level of popularity as the blacks and yellows. Originally bred to retrieve from water, the modern Labrador retriever has proven to be one of the most versatile breeds, excelling in hunt tests and field trials, in obedience and agility events, and also as service dogs.

Author Unknown

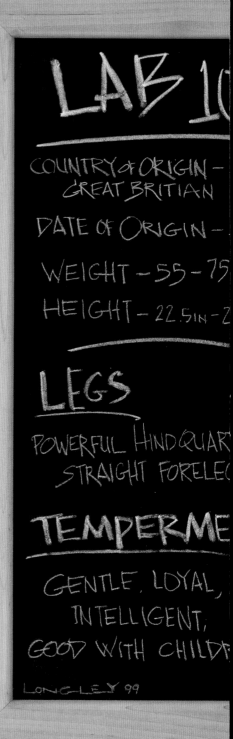

LAB 1

COUNTRY OF ORIGIN –
GREAT BRITIAN

DATE OF ORIGIN –

WEIGHT – 55 – 75

HEIGHT – 22.5 IN – 2

LEGS

POWERFUL HINDQUAR
STRAIGHT FORELE

TEMPERME

GENTLE, LOYAL,
INTELLIGENT,
GOOD WITH CHILD

LONGLEY 99

HEAD
BROAD, WITH PRONOUNCED
STOP MUZZLE OR MEDIUM LENGTH

EYES
BROWN OR HAZEL

EARS
HANG CLOSE TO
THE HEAD, SET LOW
AND FARBACK

BODY
DEEP, BROAD CHEST,
SHORT LEVEL BACK,
WIDE LOINS

TAIL
MEDIUM LENGTH,
THICKLY COVERED,
WITH NO FEATHERING

A dog teaches a boy
fidelity, perseverance,
and to turn around
three times before
lying down.
Robert Benchley

Very few things in life are as certain as the fact that if your present dog is your first Lab, it won't be your last.

Steve Smith

If you were to ask a Lab owner,
"What's it like to live with a
Lab?" he would respond with a
twinkle in his eye, "What's it
like to live without one?"

It is one thing to experience
the glory of a summer sunset
but quite another to do so with
its reflection off the eyes of a
Lab by your side.

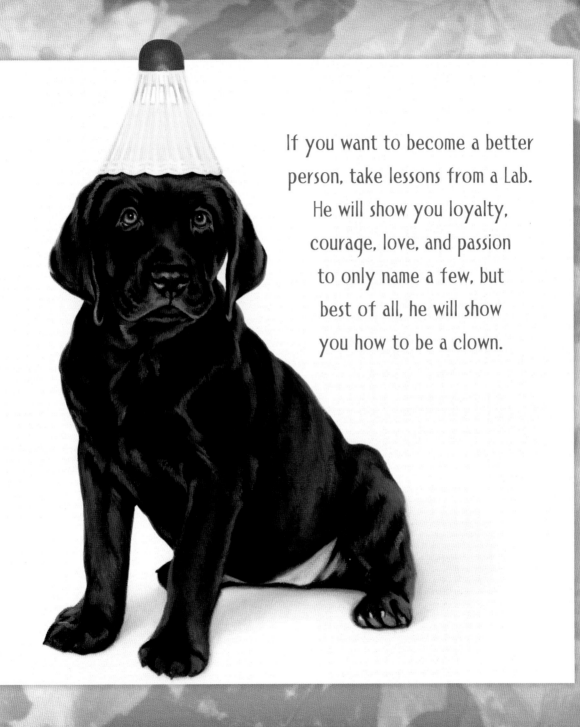

If you want to become a better person, take lessons from a Lab. He will show you loyalty, courage, love, and passion to only name a few, but best of all, he will show you how to be a clown.

You can lead a horse to water, but you can't make him drink. However, I would have to say, not only will the Lab find the water himself, but it would pretty much be impossible to keep him out of it.

When God created Labrador retrievers, He was showing off.

This same dog is also one of the most dedicated companions in the canine world, a gentle dog who is trustworthy around children and intensely devoted to its master. Labs can be trained to aid the handicapped and taught to find disaster victims in a pile of rubble. Labs can seek out drugs stashed in suitcases and find bombs hidden in buildings. They can hike for hours, camp in rugged terrain and veg out on the couch all in the same weekend. In essence, the Labrador Retriever is the consummate dog.

AUDREY PAVIA
Labrador Retriever Handbook

AMERICA'S MOST
WANTED

THE LAB GANG

ALIASES: THE CLOWN, SNEAKERS, CHECKERS, HI-JINX, STINKER, SMOOCHER . . .
CRIME: STEALING THE HEARTS OF THE AMERICAN PEOPLE AND AN OCCASIONAL TABLE SCRAP OR TWO.
CAN DISGUISE THEMSELVES IN VARIOUS COLORS.

L   R   L   R

FRONT PAWS   REAR PAWS

DATE OF BIRTH: 9/24
SEX: MALE
WEIGHT: 58 LBS.
PLACE OF BIRTH: LABRADOR
FUR COLOR: CHOCOLATE, BLACK, YELLOW
EYE COLOR: BLUE, BROWN

APPROACH WITH CAUTION

LOOKING INTO EYES MAY MELT YOUR HEART AND CAUSE ADDICTION. WATCH FOR TILTING HEAD ("THE LOOK"), YOU MUST LOOK AWAY!

ANYONE WITH INFORMATION PLEASE CALL THE PROPER AUTHORITIES

LAST SEEN CHEWING MY SHOES

$1000 REWARD

For a Lab owner the rainbow only comes
in three colors: yellow, black and chocolate.

I never met a kid who
didn't like chocolate or
a Lab that didn't love
a kid with chocolate.

I think we are drawn to
dogs because they are the
uninhibited creatures
we might be if we weren't
certain we knew better.

GEORGE BIRD EVANS

Saying that a Lab is clever may be an understatement. One best be careful not to leave him unattended in the car with the keys in the ignition.

The Labrador Retriever, America's favorite breed, is truly the dog that does it all. Labs have been valued since the breed was developed for their even temper, quick intelligence and versatility. These are lively, active sporting dogs, and there's nothing they like better than to do a job for you—whether it's retrieving a duck from a pond or your TV remote from the couch. Labs are wonderful family dogs, great with kids and sociable with others. They are also used widely as assistance dogs and in police work as bomb sniffers and drug detection dogs. The fact that Labs are so very willing to please, and enjoy working for praise, is why they are successful at just about anything they attempt. It's also why they are a very valued member of any family they join. From the dog in the White House to the dog in your yard, no other breed can fill so many niches, or please so many people with such different needs.

LISA WEISS

12

OBJECTS ARE CUTER THAN THEY APPEAR

If chocolate is an addiction,
then a chocolate Lab would
be an overdose.

There is something to be said about a pup. It has the ability to take our eyes off the busy, the things that seem to complicate this world, and bring us to a place of simplicity. It reveals to us innocence and the newness of life. It represents a new beginning, a blank page of life we are to fill with passion and excitement. It is what we make it, and the best thing is, we have no lack of space or shortness of ink.

If dogs are like candy, then the chocolate Lab is the only sweet indulgence I know that will actually help you lose weight.

Learn to walk with a Lab, and he will teach you to run. Learn to run with a Lab, and he will show you how to soar. Learn to live with a Lab, and he shall show you how to love.

16

He certainly WAS yellow. After a bath—usually compulsory—he presented a decided gamboge streak down his back, from the top of his forehead to the stump of his tail, fading in his sides and flank to a delicate straw color. His breast, legs, and feet—when not reddened by "slumgullion," in which he was fond of wading—were white. A few attempts at ornamental decoration from the India-ink pot of the storekeeper failed, partly through the yellow dog's excessive agility, which would never give the paint time to dry on him, and partly through his success in transferring his markings to the trousers and blankets of the camp.

The size and shape of his tail—which had been cut off before his introduction to Rattlers Ridge—were favorite sources of speculation to the miners, as determining both his breed and his moral responsibility in coming into camp in that defective condition. There was a general opinion that he couldn't have looked worse with a tail, and its removal was therefore a gratuitous effrontery.

His best feature was his eyes, which were a lustrous Vandyke brown, and sparkling with intelligence; but here again he suffered from evolution through environment, and their original trustful openness was marred by the experience of watching for flying stones, sods, and passing kicks from the rear, so that the pupils were continually reverting to the outer angle of the eyelid… His fondness for paddling in the ditches and "slumgullion" at one time suggested a water spaniel. He could swim, and would occasionally bring out of the river sticks and pieces of bark that had been thrown in; but as HE always had to be thrown in with them, and was a good-sized dog, his aquatic reputation faded also. He remained simply "a yaller dog." What more could be said? His actual name was "Bones"—given to him, no doubt, through the provincial custom of confounding the occupation of the individual with his quality, for which it was pointed out precedent could be found in some old English family names.

BRET HARTE
A Yellow Dog

It has been said that you can't teach an old dog new tricks, but I say a seasoned Lab can teach you a thing or two.

No matter how little money and how few possessions you own, having a dog makes you rich.

Louis Sabin

The dog represents all that is best in man.

Etienne Charlet

The Labrador, as a breed, is a friendly, happy and charming dog. Labradors are good-tempered, easy to train, eager to please, and devoted to their families. They become fond of, and attached to, other household pets, not only cats, but even hamsters and budgerigars. They will put up with almost anything from children, love their company, and are tolerant to the point of saintliness, asking for nothing more in life than to be with you and your family, and to please you all.

Heather Wiles-Fone

Some would say that a dog has the gift of reading its owner's mind, but I would say the Lab not only reads your mind but gives you his thoughts as well.

Clifford

19

If the eyes are the windows of the soul, then loyalty is the window treatment of a Lab's heart.

By the door lay another dog, nose on paws, brown eyes open and watchful in contrast to the peacefulness radiated by the other occupants of the room. This was a large red-gold Labrador retriever, a young dog with all the heritage of his sturdy working forebears in his powerful build, broad noble head and deep, blunt, gentle mouth.

SHEILA BURNFORD
The Incredible Journey

I'd rather have an inch of a dog than miles of pedigree.

DANA BURNET

21

The heart of the Lab is that of approval. He seeks and longs for it.
It is of his very being. He would pretty much
do anything to get it and give his life never to lose it.

A Lab would travel halfway
around the world in the bitter
cold only to behold that twinkle
in your eye and to hear your
voice gently speak his name.

*Dogs have given us their absolute all. We are the center of their universe.
We are the focus of their love and faith and trust. They serve us in return for
scraps. It is without a doubt the best deal man has ever made.*

Roger Caras

23

In order to really enjoy a dog,
one doesn't merely try to
train him to be semi-human.
The point of it is to open
oneself to the possibility of
becoming partly a dog.

EDWARD HOAGLAND

Dogs are pets.
Labs are family.

It would be easier to split
an atom with a butter knife
than to try and remove the
joy and passion of retrieval
from the heart of a Lab.

If puppy breath were to be bottled, the world would need not perfume anymore.

It is truly a picture to behold, the silhouette of a wet Lab kissed by the setting sun on the water's shore after a hard day of play.

To look upon a Lab pup and a young child at play, one could only but conclude that all is good in the universe.

The day after Alice died, Bella sat close to the empty bed all day. Who knows what sadness she was experiencing, but all indications were that she mourned the loss of a dear old friend. She had been through it before. Don't tell me that a dog can't teach us humans something about compassion. I saw it with my own eyes. And I believe the Lord sent this loyal Lab to comfort a woman who desperately needed encouragement through her long ordeal.

Dr. James C. Dobson

In the Lab's old age, the dog takes on many of the traits of aging humans. They exhibit a gentleness of soul you didn't know they possessed and seem to be grateful for a little attention. And even though they may still have a great zest for life and living, they are also completely aware of the exact time when the afternoon sun strikes the good couch just so, and when dinner is served.

Steve Smith

From the grayed muzzle to the worn eyes, a seasoned Lab is a tale told and a history unleashed.

29

There is something delightful, something pure, to look into the twinkle that dances in the eyes of a Lab pup.

What Can I Learn from a Lab?

Your message is simple, your example so true.

With a heart full of play, you showed us your way.

You jumped, you ran, you showed us your plan.

You gave us your best and know how to rest.

As I stare with new sight, I now have the light.

Tomorrow will come with the rising, the sun.

The lesson to do will be the art of the chew.

Now what can I say as you light up the day?

That life need not be heavy but free.

We can learn to embrace your spirit of grace.

It is with this that I say thanks all the day.

Lay your gentle head down and sweet dreams.

BRETT LONGLEY

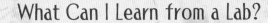

If to have a dog by your side can be defined as a simple pleasure, then a Lab by your side is a pleasure simply defined.